R. VAUGHAN WILLIAMS

FANTASIA ON SUSSEX FOLK TUNES

for Violoncello Solo and Orchestra

STUDY SCORE

MUSIC DEPARTMENT

OXFORD
UNIVERSITY PRESS

OXFORD

UNIVERSITY PRESS

Great Clarendon Street, Oxford OX2 6DP,
United Kingdom

Oxford University Press is a department of the University of Oxford.
It furthers the University's objective of excellence in research, scholarship,
and education by publishing worldwide. Oxford is a registered trade mark of
Oxford University Press in the UK and in certain other countries

This edition first published 2015

Impression: 1

ISBN 978-0-19-340773-2 (study score)
ISBN 978-0-19-369050-9 (on hire)

Music origination by Michael Durnin

Printed in Great Britain on acid-free paper by
Caligraving Ltd, Thetford, Norfolk

PREFACE

Fantasia on Sussex Folk Tunes was given its first performance by Pablo Casals, to whom it is dedicated, on 13 March 1930, at a Royal Philharmonic Society Concert conducted by John Barbirolli. The work, completed in 1929, was based on the following five folk songs: 'Salisbury Plain', 'The Long Whip', 'Low down in the broom', 'Bristol Town', and 'I've been to France'.

Although the work was on hire for a time, eventually Vaughan Williams withdrew it, having never been satisfied with it. It is not a major work, but one regrets the ban he placed on its performance. It goes some way towards disproving Lambert's oft-quoted remark that there is nothing to be done with a folk song once it has been played except to 'play it over again and play it rather louder'. Despite Lambert's *mot*, Delius in *Brigg Fair*, Vaughan Williams in several works, not to mention Dvořák, Haydn, and Beethoven, have done a great deal with variants of folk song. Vaughan Williams's rhapsodic treatment of tunes which, by their strophic nature, do not lend themselves to symphonic development, has not received its proper due in appreciation. In the *Sussex Fantasia* the tunes are extended by the composer's skill into new tunes, with an amusing commentary on the quicker tunes from the woodwind section.

Based on a note by MICHAEL KENNEDY

ORCHESTRATION

SOLO VIOLONCELLO

2 FLUTES (second doubling Piccolo)

OBOE

2 CLARINETS in B♭

2 BASSOONS

2 HORNS in F

TRUMPET in B♭

TIMPANI

STRINGS

Duration: *c*.15 minutes

Full score and orchestral parts are available on hire.

Fantasia on Sussex Folk Tunes
for
Violoncello Solo and Orchestra

R. VAUGHAN WILLIAMS

Printed in Great Britain

OXFORD UNIVERSITY PRESS, MUSIC DEPARTMENT, GREAT CLARENDON STREET, OXFORD OX2 6DP

2

4

12

16

19

23

46